WAGE WAR ON SILENCE

WAGE WAR
ON
SILENCE

A Book of Poems by

VASSAR MILLER

Wesleyan University Press

MIDDLETOWN, CONNECTICUT

Some of these poems originally appeared in magazines or anthologies, and some in the author's previous book, *Adam's Footprint*. Grateful acknowledgment is made to the editors of the following publications: *The Gusher, A Houyhnhm's Scrapbook, Janus, The New-England Galaxy* (Old Sturbridge Inc.), *New Orleans Poetry Journal, New World Writing* (May 1957), *Paris Review, Prairie Schooner, The Provincial, Southwest Review,* and *Texas Quarterly.*

Library of Congress Catalog Card Number: 60–13157.
Manufactured in the United States of America.
First edition.

For Daryl

Contents

III

WAGE WAR ON SILENCE

Without Ceremony

Except ourselves, we have no other prayer;
Our needs are sores upon our nakedness.
We do not have to name them; we are here.
And You who can make eyes can see no less.
We fall, not on our knees, but on our hearts,
A posture humbler far and more downcast;
While Father Pain instructs us in the arts
Of praying, hunger is the worthiest fast.
We find ourselves where tongues cannot wage war
On silence (farther, mystics never flew)
But on the common wings of what we are,
Borne on the wings of what we bear, toward You,
Oh Word, in whom our wordiness dissolves,
When we have not a prayer except ourselves.

I

Prayer Against Two Perils

How may your poor child, father, dare surmise
The shape of grief your death would wear, or know
How tears, once wasted over trifles, flow
(If storms of agony do not capsize
Custom's old crates), or how these very eyes
Should gaze along a road you did not go?
But since all means are impotent to show,
All means save one, may you not make me wise.

Yet if, most erudite in pain and loss
From measuring barefoot, jag by jag, their earth,
You swear the lack of me deserves your bother
Or dream such dismal desert fit to cross,
Your blood splashed over clods of fancied worth,
May I not make you wise, poor child, my father.

Christmas Mourning

On Christmas Day I weep
Good Friday to rejoice.
I watch the Child asleep.
Does He half dream the choice
The Man must make and keep?

At Christmastime I sigh
For my Good Friday hope.
Outflung the Child's arms lie
To span in their brief scope
The death the Man must die.

Come Christmastide I groan
To hear Good Friday's pealing.
The Man, racked to the bone,
Has made His hurt my healing,
Has made my ache His own.

Slay me, pierced to the core
With Christmas penitence
So I who, new-born, soar
To that Child's innocence,
May wound the Man no more.

The New Icarus

Slip off the husk of gravity to lie
Bedded with wind; float on a whimsy, lift
Upon a wish: your bow's own arrow, rift
Newton's decorum—only when you fly.
But naked. No false-feathered fool, you try
Dalliance with heights, nor, plumed with metal, shift
And shear the clouds, imperiling lark and swift
And all birds bridal-bowered in the sky.

Your wreck of bone, barred their delight's dominions,
Lacking their formula for flight, holds imaged
Those alps of air no eagle's wing can quell.
With arms flung crosswise, pinioned to wooden pinions,
You, in one motion plucked and crimson-plumaged,
Outsoar all Heaven, plummeting all Hell.

Adam's Footprint

Once as a child I loved to hop
On round plump bugs and make them stop
Before they crossed a certain crack.
My bantam brawn could turn them back,
My crooked step wrenched straight to kill
Live pods that then screwed tight and still.

Small sinner, stripping boughs of pears,
Shinnied past sweet and wholesome airs,
How could a tree be so unclean?
Nobody knows but Augustine.
He nuzzled pears for dam-sin's dugs—
And I scrunched roly-poly bugs.

No wolf's imprint or tiger's trace
Does Christ hunt down to catch with grace
In nets of love the devious preys
Whose feet go softly all their days:
The foot of Adam leaves the mark
Of some child scrabbling in the dark.

Autumnal Spring Song

When autumn wounds the bough
And bleeds me white and shaken,
Forbear to tell me how
The spring must reawaken
  And the trees bloom on forever,
  But with the same leaves never.

When autumn smears the sheen
Of leaf-lace, nature's lore
Affirms each season's green
To shimmer as before
  While the trees bloom on forever.
  But with the same leaves? Never.

When every branch is whole
The bitter sword of spring
Will scar the forest's soul
And mine remembering
  That the trees bloom on forever,
  But with the same leaves never.

Lord, You must comfort me
When woods are autumn's spoil,
Yet with another Tree
Unnourished by the soil
  Whence the trees bloom on forever,
  But with the same leaves never.

Invocation to Bacchus Grown Old

Come weave me out of wine
A fabric frail and fine;
Come wrap me well within
Its bubble's rosy skin
So delicate a breath
May tear its tender sheath,
With me so poised past stir
No darker sepulchre
Could bury me deep under
The earth from snarl of thunder.
Since on its fragile woof
The ancient stamp of hoof,
Though light as dewdrop's clatter
Would, beating, bruise and shatter;
Since you and I and time
Have worn away our prime
Beyond all tug of lust
In either groin or ghost
Wherefore the grape is broken
In low or lofty token;
Since we're too old to leap—
No prayer of mine shall keep
Your ear except for sleep.

Crone's Cradle-Song

Hushed hands, before you fumble
Into knot and gnarl,
Fixed feet, before you stumble
Weaving steps asnarl—
  Much prefer
   Stillness without stir.

Mute mouth, before you break
Song against your tongue,
Lax lips, before you make
Music wried-and-wrung—
  Silence dance
   Down such dissonance!

Body, before you race
Brain and blood and breath
Against the grain of grace,
Bend birth back to death—
  Lullaby,
   Given leave to die.

Beside a Deathbed

Her spirit hiding among skin and bones
In willingness and wariness waits death
Like hares that peer from corners of their pens
Lured by a curiosity, yet loath.
Her eyes meet bed, chair, face, but do not focus,
As if these objects, heretofore mere shade,
Have caught up with their shadows. Things that wake us
Upon her eyelids heap a heavy load.
As straws pierce rock, our words reach where she lies,
Heedless of our cheerfulness or condolence.
Uncaring how our chatter ebbs or flows,
She catches the first syllable of silence.
So true the craftsman, memory, in lying
She will be less a stranger dead than dying.

Bout With Burning

awareness of physical suffering (handwritten annotation)

I have tossed hours upon the tides of fever,
Upon the billows of my blood have ridden,
Where fish of fancy teem as neither river
Nor ocean spawns from India to Sweden.
Here while my boat of body burnt has drifted
Along her sides crawled tentacles of crabs
Sliming her timbers; on the waves upwafted
Crept water rats to gnaw her ropes and ribs.
Crashing, she has dived, her portholes choking
With weed and ooze, the swirls of black and green
Gulping her inch by inch, the seagulls' shrieking
Sieved depth through depth to silence. Till blast-blown,
I in my wreck beyond storm's charge and churning
Have waked marooned upon the coasts of morning.

15

Columbus Dying

His men in fever, scabs, and hunger pains—
He found a world and put to scorn his scorners.
Yet having learned the living sea contains
No dragons gnawing on drowned sailors' brains,
He missed the angels guarding the four corners,
And begged that he be buried with his chains

In token that he'd sworn to serve as thrall
His vision of men creeping to and fro,
Gum-footed flies glued to a spinning ball.
Whether they tumble off earth's edge or crawl
Till dropped dead in their tracks from vertigo,
He deemed would make no difference at all.

Fantasy on the Resurrection

Flaws cling to flesh as dews cling to a rose:
The cripples limp as though they would prolong,
Walking, a waltz; the deaf ears, opened, close
As if their convolutions hoard all song;
The blind eyes keep half shut as if to fold
A vision fast men never glimpse by staring;
Against their will the mute lips move that hold
A language which was never tongue's for sharing.
Shocked shag of earth and everything thereunder
Turned inside out—the nail-gnarled have caught Heaven
Like a bright ball. Not in their reknit wonder,
But in their wounds lies Christ's sprung grace engraven—
Not in the body lighter than word spoken,
But in the side still breached, the hands still broken.

Reciprocity

You who would sorrow even for a token
Of hurt in me no less than you would grieve
For seeing me with my whole body broken
And long no less to solace and relieve;
You who, as though you wished me mere Good Morning,
Would smash your heart upon the hardest stones
Of my distress as when you once, unscorning,
Would sleep upon the margin of my moans—
I yield my want, this house of gutted portals,
All to your want, I yield this ravaged stack,
In testimony that between two mortals
No gift may be except a giving back.
What present could I make you from what skill
When your one need is me to need you still?

Unspoken Dialogue

Mine was a question I could never ask;
Yours was the answer you could never tell.
Our conversation hid behind the mask
Of reticence. Death having cleaved our shell
Of silence, silence was our core as well.

You had a secret, one you longed to share
In vain because my muteness was the sieve
Through which it slipped. Yet you who could not spare
Breath to explain, but only breath to live,
You were the secret you could never give.

Neither my question nor your answer matters;
The promise is unkept, the miracle
Unwrought, the song uncaroled, since it shatters
Sooner than shaped. For in heart's tongue-tied lull
The word unspoken proves unspeakable.

For One Long Dead

Death broke the habit such as binds
A life to one unlovely spot;
So, from the corner of our minds
We glimpsed your going—then forgot.

Yet we, not you, have gone the ways
Of ghosts, not one of whom endures
For you, since God's consuming gaze
Has burned our memory from yours.

The Final Hunger

Hurl down the nerve-gnarled body hurtling head-
Long into sworls of shade-hush. Plummeting, keep
The latch of eyelids shut to so outleap
Care's claws. Arms, legs, abandon grace and spread
Your spent sprawl—glutton ravening to be fed
With fats, creams, fruits, meats, spice that heavy-heap
The hands, that golden-gloss the flesh, of sleep,
Sleep, the sole lover that I take to bed.

But they couch crouching in the darkness, city
Of wakefulness uncaptured by assaulting—
Senses by sleep unravished and unwon.
Sun-sword night-sheathed, lie never between (have pity!)
Between me and my love, between me and the vaulting
Down the dense sweetness of oblivion.

Faintly and From Far Away

Between the wheeze of her torpor and the wind of her falling,
Between the whey of her face and the snow of its blanching,
Between the vacuum of her monotone and the void of its stilling
Was only the difference between the cicadas on a summer after-
        noon
And their declining into the bottom of evening,
Only the difference between the sparrows pecking the rock of
        silence
And the rock of silence itself.

Father, rememberer of sparrows and dullards,
Each of us cries, even as she, from some twig of a cross:
     Remember me, Lord. Before it swoops me up, feather
     The hawk of the world's forgetting with the down of
     Your memory.

No Return

Once over summer streams the ice-crusts harden,
No one can wade therein to wash his feet
Thence to go flying after nymphs that fleet
Naked and nimble through the woods. Time's warden
Has locked them all (or is it us?) past pardon.
Yet freed, we could not find the path that beat
Toward—call it any name—fauns, home, retreat;
For there is no returning to that garden.

No, not to Adam's. We must keep our own,
Remembering. In Eden's greenery
God walked. While in our garden rocks are brown
With His dried blood where He has crouched to groan.
Our apples rotted, only His crosstree
Bears crimson fruit. But no hand plucks it down.

Paradox

Mild yoke of Christ, most harsh to me not bearing,
You bruise the neck that balks, the hands that break you;
Sweet bread and wine, bitter to me not sharing,
You scar and scorch the throat that will not take you;
Mount where He taught, you cripple feet not bloody
From your sharp flints of eight-fold benediction;
Bright cross, most shameful stripped of the stripped body,
You crucify me safe from crucifixion:
Yet I, who am my own dilemma, jolting
My mind with thought lest it unthink its stiffness,
Rise to revolt against my own revolting.
Blind me to blindness, deafen me to deafness.
So will Your gifts of sight and hearing plunder
My eyes with lightning and my ears with thunder.

II

Inviolate

Too long lies the will virgin where she sleeps
Under the room of mind adept at dancing
His gambados upon his floor, entrancing
Attention from the cubicle which keeps
Her flower on ice; however goat-heart leaps
To his own syncopations, so commencing
Flirtations with High Heaven, his lewd prancing
Does not disturb the slumberer in the deeps.

Yet her dead brain is its own troubled dream,
The chill of her body being a frost in blaze,
Her strict gown but a frozen gust. Wherefore,
Swift fingers, rend it, seam from crystal seam;
Bruise, burn, and bare the plump peace of her glaze
Till she lies cradled, cooled, and clothed in fire.

Receiving Communion

The world of stars and space being His bauble,
>   He gives me, not a toy
>   which were I to destroy
would be no waste that caused Him any trouble,
rather, into my fingers cramped and crooked
>   entrusts His body real
>   as spitted on a nail
as are my own hands piteous, naked—
because He has no creaking heart's mill grind
>   His wheat, nor heart's belief
>   play oven; for His loaf
cannot be beaten out or baked by hand—
when He, against the mind's backlash,
>   would as a splinter list
>   here on my turbulent dust
preventing so all fantasy of flesh.

Cacophony

Her bed as narrow as a cross, she lies
Each night and offers Christ her twisted cries;
But He who has not blessed the soul to plague
The body, has not fitted a round peg
Into a square hole; so, He tells her what
Of old He said to Mary, "Touch Me not,

"If you would keep that which you would enjoy,
For flesh embracing spirit must destroy
Itself, too impotent for what demands
A more tenacious grip than clutching hands.
And, stripping, you remove the wrong robes till
You have undone the buttons of self-will."

So, while the incense of her sighs shall mingle
With sweat, her yearning eye is pure and single
For homely lust as little as for God,
Since, if one night the boilings of her blood
Drowned her devotions, dawn would find her fled,
Cramped by a love no wider than her bed.

Ballad of the Unmiraculous Miracle

Sit under a pine on Christmas Eve,
Heart bruised like a fallen nestling,
And the angels will sing you—no song save
The wind in the branches wrestling.

Peer down a mystical well and see
Far down in its waters mirrored—
The only sign there imaged for me,
My own face mournful and harrowed.

Seek out a stable known of old
And see the oxen kneel—
With me crouched here before the cold
And hunger sharp as steel.

Go wander through the winter snows
And spy the Christmas bud
Unfold itself—the only rose
The brambles bear, my blood.

Like wingless birds are wind and wood,
Well, oxen, flowering bush
Till Christmas Day when I see God
Plumaged in my plucked flesh.

Bethlehem Outcast

Is there no warmth to heal me any more,
Straining to glimpse His manger, clutched by chills
Upon the lintel of the stable door;

Thawed by His breath, the oxen foul the floor,
While through my reedy bones the north wind shrills:
Is there no warmth to heal me any more?

Darkward His radiance reaches to explore
All nights but one whose shudder never stills
Upon the lintel of the stable door

Through which the gutturals of shepherds soar
In flight with singing star-bursts from the hills.
Is there no warmth to heal me any more?

Watching the magi yield Him royal store,
I wait held back and bound between two wills
Upon the lintel of the stable door.

Christ, save this wiseman without winter lore,
This bumpkin naked to the cold that kills!
Is there no warmth to heal me any more
Upon the lintel of the stable door?

A Duller Moses

I litter Heaven with myself, a wad
Of tedium tossed into it, debris
Marring the skyscape wherein nebulae
Have shuddered into worlds, which at His nod
Shiver as swiftly into ash. I doze and do not see
How on time's bramble bush impaling me
Each moment is a thorn aflame with God,
Burning within, without me night and day.
I tremble, dreaming between sleep and sleep
That He, both radiance and incendiary,
In my heart lies as on the cross He lay
(Which bed is fouler?), making my bone-heap—
Oh, monstrous miracle!—God's sanctuary.

Second Rate

With numb, invisible face
I wander up and down;
By less than half a pace
Betraying that the tune

Is pain's beneath the bandage
Pulsing, I comport
Myself to bear its bondage
As if I felt no hurt

Dealt by a blade that swerves
But halfway to the grain,
Scraping across the nerves
Thin echoes from the bone

Ebbing simply because
Today dies in tomorrow;
Yet none of nature's laws
Allays this subtler sorrow

The saints, whose wounds He honors
God rallies to their prime,
But delegates us sinners
His cold assistant, Time.

Love's Risk

(For Katherine)

Is there such a thing as love without faith?
Doubt . . . is a consequence of the risk of faith.
—Tillich

She is elusive like the wind,
So is she fugitive like air,
Yet since you'd stifle for the want
Of breath, she'll come back, never fear.
For though you'll trap her in no fence,
Love's meshes will, but do not ask her whence.

Her heart that yields to all who ache
And scorns to bask upon its shelf
Reserves the secret by whose roots
Her heart lies hidden in itself.
None ravels out her reticence:
She's her own gift, but do not ask her whence.

She is as durable as oak,
She is resilient as a pine;
So, knock upon her as you will;
Yet he whose measure dared define
Her core would work her violence;
You'll see her soon, but do not ask her whence.

She stops by every lonely house,
Where no dark pain can scare her out;
Yet, building her a room within
Your faith, leave her a door of doubt
As risk, rare touch of excellence,
And she'll return, but do not ask her whence.

A Lesson in Detachment

She's learned to hold her gladness lightly,
Remembering when she was a child
Her fingers clenched a bird too tightly,
And its plumage, turned withered leaf,
No longer fluttered wild.

Sharper than bill or claw, her grief
Needled her palm that ached to bleed,
And could not, to assuage the grief
Pulsations of the tiny scrap
Crumpled against her need.

To prison love: a tiny snap
Of iron to be forged a band,
A toy to prove one day a trap
Destined to close without a qualm
Upon itself, her hand.

She bids her clutching five grow calm
Lest in their grip a wing might buckle
Beyond repair, and for her balm
She'll cup no joy now in her palm,
But perch it on her knuckle.

Song for a Marriage

Housed in each other's arms,
Thatched with each other's grace,
Your bodies, flint on steel
Striking out fire to fend
The cold away awhile;
With sweat for mortar, brace
Your walls against the sleet
And the rib-riddling wind.

A house, you house yourselves,
Housed, you will house another,
Scaled to a subtler blueprint
Than architects can draw—
A triple function yours
In this world's winter weather,
Oh, breathing brick and stone,
I look on you with awe.

A fig for praise that calls
Flesh a bundle of sticks,
Kindling for flame that feels
Like swallowing the sun!
Yet luxury turned labor's
No old maid's rancid mix,
But how bone-masonry
Outweighs the skeleton.

For a Christening

(For my first nephew)

Like the first man to glance
Into a face and fathom
The word as welcome, dance
The common human rhythm;
Like all fish or fawn that came
At Adam's cry, or dove—
So you are what we name,
And what we name we love.

Or like the stars recorded
By shepherds who had striven
With wonder and thus worded
The wilderness of heaven,
Shy creature growing tame,
Taken from womb's dense grove—
You now are what we name
When what we name we love.

One with all precious things
Called from the dusk of death,
Rose-texture, whir of wings,
Garrisoned with our breath—
You wear its sheath of flame
Around, beneath, above
You, being what we name
For you are what we love.

One with the sacred powers
Man cradles on his tongue
During time's timeless hours
Whereon his heart is hung—

In the adoring frame
Made by our arms, you move;
For you are what we name,
And what we name we love.

In the Name of the Three in One,
More awesome still than yours,
From whence your mystery spun,
Wherein it yet endures,
Speaking, though holy shame
Would silence us, we prove
How what we love we name
How what we name we love!

Joyful Prophecy

(For Daryl)

If he is held in love,
the thin reeds of my baby's bones
are pipes for it, it hums

and chuckles from the hollows
as a flower whispers,
it ripples off him, suave

honey of the sunlight
stored for his kin, his kind, such lovely
mirrors of it, he

is tempted to hoard it in
his well where he may gaze at it,
yet held in love and gracious

he shares it with his sister;
but, lest death waste it on the wind,
love measures him for the man

who can hold its heartiness
fermented to a man's delight,
if he is held in love.

The Whooping Crane

Observe the Whooping Crane
Who still enjoys the weather
Despite his wingdom's wane—
A bird of different feather.

Less amorous advance
Than art unparagoned,
His swirling, sweeping dance
Becomes a saraband,

To which he dedicates
Devotion so austere
His most attuned of mates
Lays but an egg a year.

He counts it bliss, not bother,
That less than half a dozen
Make free to call him father
Or even claim him cousin.

Love Song for the Future

To our ruined vineyards come,
Little foxes, for your share
Of our blighted grapes, the tomb
Readied for our common lair.
Ants, we open you the cupboard;
Flee no more the heavy hand
Harmless as a vacant scabbard
Since our homes like yours are sand.

Catamounts so often hunted,
Wend your ways through town or city,
Since both you and we are haunted
By the Weird Ones with no pity.
Deer and bear we used to stalk,
We would spend our dying pains
Nestling you with mouse and hawk
Near our warmth until it wanes.

Weave across our faces, spiders,
Webwork fragile as a flower;
Welcome, serpents, subtle gliders,
For your poison fails in power.
Loathed no longer, learn your worth,
Toad and lizard, snail and eel—
Remnants of a living earth
Cancelled by a world of steel,

Whose miasmic glitter dances
Over beast's and man's sick daze
While our eyes which scorned St. Francis
Watch Isaiah's vision craze:
Ox and lion mingling breath
Eat the straw of doom; in tether
To the selfsame stake of death
Wolf and lamb lie down together.

Lullaby for a Grown Man

Laced in your shell of sleep,
Lie here secure from sorrow
And dread and need to weep
Till hatched anew tomorrow.
Returned to egg, strange bird,
When fetal slumber gathers
You to itself, unstirred
Cling to the night-hen's feathers.

I will her my own breast
So—lighter than a thought
Hovered over your nest—
Warming your nest of nought,
No wings may ever scatter
One twig of it where lingers
Your shell forespun to scatter
Between the sun's lank fingers.

In the Fullness of Time

I am heavy with my wait
Through each moment's long-drawn sigh
While my heart, my drowsy strummer
Plays my body tunes of calm.
I am somnolent with fate,
Gaze with animal's soft eye,
Take the humid strokes of summer
On a saint's extended palm.

Singled out, and one of many,
I have paid the selfsame debt
Of a princess frail for bearing
Of a field hand tumbled down.
I am common as a penny,
Costly as a coronet,
Pushed out of sight and mind and caring,
Comforted in peacock's down.

Pangs of glory soon must dig
Through my yielding bone their furrow
Depths of which can never measure
What I have to cultivate—
Whether rose or twisted twig;
To my joy or to my sorrow
Lying here past pain and pleasure,
I am heavy with my wait.

In Consolation

Do I love you? The question might be well
Rephrased, What do I love? Your face?
Suppose it twisted to a charred grimace.
Your mind? But if it turned hospital cell,
Though pity for its inmate might compel
Sick calls from time to time, I should embrace
A staring stranger whom I could not place.
So, cease demanding what I cannot tell

Till He who made you shows me where He keeps you,
And not some shadow of you I pursue
And, having found, have only flushed a wraith.
Nor am I Christ to cleave the dark that steeps you.
He loves you then, not I— Or if I do,
I love you only by an act of faith.

The Quarry

What are you, then, my love, my friend, my father,
My anybody-never-mine? Whose aim
Can wing you with a knowledge-bullet, tame
You long enough to term you fur or feather?
Labeled one species, you become another
Before I have pronounced your latest name.
My fingers itching after you, like flame
Melting to frost, you vanish into neither.

Face, mind, heart held in honor for your sake,
Magical creature none can ever snare,
Are but the trails you beat, the arcs you make,
Shy animal the color of the air,
Who are the air itself, the breath ashake
Among the leaves—the bird no longer there.

How Far?

How far is it to you by foot?
Ten thousand stones,
Two million grains of dust and soot,
All my bruised bones.

How far is it to you by sea?
Twelve hills and hollows
Of water, each one risking me
Gulped in salt swallows.

How far is it to you by rail?
A myriad meadows
Sweeping the window in a gale
Of golden shadows.

How far is it to you by air?
Ten thousand thunders,
Countless ice crystals set aflare
With rainbow wonders.

How far is it to you by light?
Two parted petals
Of eyelids flowering with sight
Where sunshine settles.

How far is it to you by love?
I have no notion.
For so to seek and find you prove
One selfsame motion.

Shifty Eyes

Your eyes, brown timid sparrows, rove,
Made wary of all resting places,
Yet seeking out a nest of love
Among the branches of our faces.

When you forsook a little while
Your dartings on that summer day
To rest a moment on my smile
Then of a sudden flew away,

Leaving your half-built nest all scattered
Because you felt a sunbeam prickle,
Because some shadow had you fluttered—
I did you ill to call you fickle,

You whose brief safety in the air
You barter for a brittle glance,
Who teeter on a curious stare
Requiring constant vigilance.

The Worshiper

Her eyes long hollowed out to pits for shadow,
Her cheeks sucking in darkness, forever making
A face at sorrow, phantom desperado,
Haunting as she is haunted, bent on taking
A stranglehold upon it to cry, "Look."
That we no more may scoff in answer, "Where?"—
She kneels and, shuddered down into the cloak
Of silence, rears her fragile walls from prayer
And music, candle, creed, and psalter
Where she may tell upon her beads her seven
Most dolorous mysteries. Above her altar
Stern Witnesses who one time crashed to Heaven
Out of their flesh's glory-gutted hull
Turn from her, being also pitiful.

The Tree of Silence

(For Nancy)

Upon the branches of our silence hang our words,
Half-ripened fruit.
Gone are the months of summer, gone
Beyond pursuit.
Let us leave, though pinched and wan,
The windfalls wither
Under the tree whose shade affords
No shelter either.

For when was language ever food for human yearning!
Sun-gilded rain
Mocking the sheen of golden peach,
Words only drain
Hearts of strength; let mortal speech
Make time and way
For life, the long and lonely learning
How to pray.

Hunger

The hour seized by the nape,
We meet with joy, yet grope
For speech, too soft a shape
For hunger honed on hope.

Our time together ends,
Leaving us drab and dry
As though only two winds
Had passed each other by.

So with the grace God offers,
It fades like seeds unsprung
Or the communion wafer's
Faint sweetness from the tongue.

Both moments must escape
Down the horizon's slope
Cast in their shadow shape
For hunger honed on hope.

With either moment vanished,
The grief-pressed heart might smother,
Were not each pain diminished
In mirroring the other.

Dialogue on Dire Possibilities

"Who'll wrench the rock
That breaks the flow
Of mind?" "How much
An hour?" "Oh, no!

"Love is not love
That asks a price,
For love is gift
And sacrifice."

"Yet with what right
Have you the hope
That any heart
Can have such scope?

"Would not the shoulders
That dared take
The burden of
Your being break?"

"Yet I must empty
All this load,
Or die. Where then?"
"The deeps of God."

"What if I fail
To swing my gate
Out toward them? Or,
Of its own weight,

"If it should close
And, closed, should swell."
"What else have wise men
Meant by Hell?"

The Common Core

Each man's sorrow is an absolute
Each man's pain is a norm
No one can prove and no one refute.
Which is the blacker, coal or soot?
Which blows fiercer, gale or storm?
Each man's sorrow is an absolute.

No man's sickness has a synonym,
No man's disease has a double.
You weep for your love, I for my limbs—
Who mourns with reason? who over whims?
For, self-defined as a pebble,
No man's sickness has a synonym.

Gangrene is fire and cancer is burning.
Which one's deadlier? Toss
A coin to decide; past your discerning
Touch the heart's center, still and unturning,
That common core of the Cross;
You die of fire and I die of burning.

Old Man

My memories slip my mind as water pouring
Runs through the fingers of a child,
More briefly held, more swiftly tiring,
For I am old.

My thoughts, like children in a magic thicket,
Stumble in search as each new trail
Is lost in briars that overtake it
More densely still.

Yet children's wits are like young boughs that ripple
To pleasure you who train them, subtle
As mine are not. For theirs, how supple!
And mine, how brittle!

So that you lay as bright foil to their promise
Their clumsy gambol, graceful error,
But curse my blunder on the premise
That I, old horror,

Have veins where time goes running wild and laughs
Mocking at me who would proscribe it
In vain, addicted so to life's
Unhealthy habit.

Carmel: Impression

High over the gasp of the waters
And hard by the hawk of the gull
Echoing through gullies and gutters
Of wind down the rain's drifting wall,

Here the harpy hatches her egg
In the nest of my turrets whereon
Ever flies the flag of the fog
Against the mean eyelids of men——

How often in dreams I have spelt
Man's epitaph red in the froth
Of his blood or tasted in salt
Of this air clean tang of his death!

For his language has sullied the sheen
Of silence like the storm-eagle's croak,
And he plucks to a brittle bone
Pure fury with thought's probing beak.

My flesh, having drunk through its sponge
Far-off fetors of man's ennui,
Would vomit itself in a plunge
To the turbulent peace of the sea.

The Logic of Silence

I left my heart
By chance uncased
For any to saw
Without a qualm
When, found of you,
Its pulses raced,
Melting to music
In your palm,

Wherein it throbbed
Like waters shaking
And, wafted like foam
Upon their sweep,
My mind from stillness
Sometimes waking
Flowed into words
On back to sleep.

Now I move heavily
To that tune,
Teased with its words
Whose splintered chips
Massed by its tide
Into the bone
Deadlock love's weight
Against my lips.

Return

From what I am, to be what I am not,
To be what once I was, from plan and plot
To learn to take no thought,
I go, my God, to Thee.

With act of faith whose throes and throbs convulse
My heart as if all other acts were else
Than dyings, prayer than pulse,
I go, my God, to Thee.

On feet thread through by seams of blood and fire,
Dancing the narrow pathway, strictest wire,
As butterflies a briar,
I go, my God, to Thee.

To balance like a bird with wings aflare,
Pinned to the cross as though I merely were
Stenciled by light on air,
I go, my God, to Thee.

My spirit, trim, uncorseted from stress,
Stripping to wind and sunlight, to the grace
Of Eden's nakedness
Will go, my God, to Thee.

The Resolution

You broke Your teeth upon the question Why,
Sucking its acrid marrow dry,
Its taste of silence wry.

Like You, on quandaries ripened in the brain,
Dropped on the heart, I bruised in vain;
Poised on this point of pain,

We find no room, whether at odds like fencers,
We two, or in embrace like dancers,
For questions or for answers

Except ourselves when, I in You, for once
The query rests in the response,
The candle in its sconce.

"Though He Slay Me"

Still tell me no, my God, and tell me no
Till I repeat the syllable for a song,
Or hold it when my mouth is cracked like clay
Cold for a pebble underneath my tongue;
Or to my comfort as my father's stir
In sleep once solaced my child's heart that knew
Although he did not waken he was near,
Still tell me no, my God, still tell me no
And, opening thus the wound that will never heal
Save torn once more, as Jacob's in his thigh,
Chafed by the hand that dealt it, was made whole,
Still tell me no, my God, still tell me no
Until I hear in it only the hush
Between Good Friday's dusk and Easter Day,
The lullaby that locked his folded lash—
I lulled to a like darkness with Your no,
No, no, still no, the echo of Your yes
Distorted among the crevices and caves
Of the coiled ear which deep in its abyss
Resolves to music all Your negatives.

III

The Healing Light

(For a friend)

You felt I would not harm you, dutiful
As I had been, yet love must strip to love.
Love must be sure and yet it cannot prove,
If it would yield us, not alone its soul,
But bait our need with its frail body, whence
We learn love's name is not expedience.

You felt I would not harm you, who remembered
How love at first was terror until it
Taught us wild children terror's opposite
And when we saw, upon love's heart we summered,
Guiltless, yet till then love must bare its side
Against the truth that love is crucified.

You felt I would not harm you, yet you trembled
A little to recall what wise men know:
That love must be a fool and dare not show
Its wisdom save as darkness and dissembled
Into the hideous riddle that is Hell
And where its children fall descend as well.

Offering: For All My Loves

This vessel take—
No chalice and no goblet,
Nothing so picturesque as a gourd
Or an oaken bucket,
But more like a rusty can
Kicked up from the dirt
Buckled and bent and warped,
Yet filled with the liquor of lightning,
The same as distilled from the flowers of children,
From the arbors of home,
From the wild grapes of martyrs, trampled for Christ,
Or as mixed with the solder of music,
With the webwax of words,
The same and no different,
Only shaped to misshapenness
In a hunk of corroded tin,
Hold me with care and decorum
For a little but not too long
Lest my jagged edge cut you,
My acrid drip scald you,
Etching a crooked shadow
On the lip of your proper love.

Conquered

Were my thoughts leashes,
they would draw me to you;
were my thoughts chains,
they would bind you to my heart;
were my thoughts kings,
they could command you.
Yet you cheat me of my anger
with your gentleness,
making my thoughts children
that sit around you,
flowers wilting and waiting
the dews of your attention.
For you do not wound my silence
with a sound,
but beyond word or act
bless me with your being.

Unnecessary

With your coming
the words I have arranged
stumble like year-old children,
my thoughts scattered
like flustered pullets.
And yet your footfall does not sway
a single leaf enough to jostle
one atom of air from another.
Indeed, my silence
summons you as well,
my need so woven into your nature
no hands pluck apart the threads,
no ear discerns my asking from your answer.
I need as much to beg
the earth to turn
or God to be.

For Instruction

Teach me some prayer
tender as you are tender when
one of my shadows mingles with one of yours and makes
an intricate weave we walk on for a moment,
gentle as you are gentle when
you humble yourself to take my kiss,
wordless as we are wordless when
a pause has fallen between us like a petal.

Comparisons

You are like roses growing,
and I with a sense for your fragrance
would be gracious as you and not rob
the air of one petal.
Still forgive me if sometimes
you are like a drink of cold water,
and I, whose thirst is an anger,
cannot get enough.
Yet you will forgive, for, remember
how once your No was so gentle
it was more like a Yes,
with your hands in my hair
making a music that only
my heart heard?
So, in the end you are like
a song I go singing.

Defense Rests

I want
a love to hold
in my hand because love
is too much for the heart to bear
alone.

Then stop
mouthing to me
"Faith and Sacraments" when
the Host feather-heavy weighs down
my soul.

So I
blaspheme! My Lord,
John's head on your breast or
Mary's lips on your feet, would you
agree?

If this
is not enough—
upon Your sweat, Your thirst,
Your nails, and nakedness I rest
my case.